CREATING A SUCCESSFUL BUSINESS ONLINE

How to Harness the Power of the Internet to
Create a Profitable Business

Curtis Wilbur

Copyright © 2017 Curtis Wilbur
All rights reserved.
ISBN-10: 1979538301
ISBN-13: 978-1979538305

Contents

Section One: How to Begin 7

    Chapter One: Setting Goals 8
    Chapter Two: Commitment 16

Section Two: Developing Your Brand on the Online Market 25

    Chapter Three: The Online Business Market 26
    Chapter Four: Developing a Personal Brand 36
    Chapter Five: Working with Your Customers 43

Section Three: Markets 51

    Chapter Six: The Amazon Market 52
    Chapter Seven: The YouTube Market 58
    Chapter Eight: The Blogging Market 69
    Chapter Nine: The Freelance Market 75

Section Four: Start Your Business 80

    Chapter Ten: Choosing Your Niche 81
    Chapter Eleven: Framing Your Business for Success 89

SECTION ONE:
How to Begin

Chapter One:
Setting Goals

Picture your life in twenty-five years. Where do you live? How big is your house? What kind of car do you drive? Are you married? Do you have children, and if so, how many? Where do you travel? Are you working or are you retired?

Hopefully you have some picture in your head of what your life in twenty-five years should look like. From this point forward, everything you do, every action you make, should be in service of this perfect future you have imagined.

This is the first step to your journey to success. You must have some ultimate goal that you look forward to down the road that constantly refocuses you on the right track to success. If all we see when we think of success are dollar signs and nothing tangible, then you will find it difficult to truly be successful.

Many entrepreneurs use the image of owning a sports car as a starting block for their journey to success. They want to buy a Lamborghini or a Ferrari, which serve as something they can work towards as they develop their business and begin making money. While this may seem like a ridiculous thing to be working towards, it works for some people, and it might even work for you. It is essential to have that goal in mind as it will help to keep you oriented toward success.

Now the line between your goals and your ultimate success can sometimes be blurred. You may make $1 Million by the end of this year and be able to buy that Lamborghini or the beach house you've wanted all your life, but remember that you have not found success until you achieve all your goals and are able to do everything you've ever wanted to do. This is, in essence, what success is: being able to fulfill every single goal that you set for yourself.

If the only goal you set for yourself is owning a Lamborghini you will end up lonely, depressed, unfulfilled, and most likely not very wealthy. You must set many goals for yourself, and only once you have achieved every one of those goals can you finally call yourself successful.

Unfortunately, most people won't be successful. They might be able to achieve some of their goals in life, most people will eventually get married, have children, and live in a nice house with a couple of cars, but very few will own the house of their dreams, send their children to the best schools, start that charity they've always wanted, or be able to retire at fifty. Even fewer will own a business they truly enjoy, live on the private island of their dreams, and travel the world in a private jet, staying at five-star hotels everywhere they go. But some, of course, will be able to do every one of these things and more, and it all lies in their ability to make goals and constantly reorient themselves in the pursuit of their goals.

The biggest barrier to success is not being able to see your goals clearly. As we have already learned, setting goals is essential to success, as it allows us something to look forward to down the road. As an entrepreneur this is even more critical to your success. There will be many days where you work for eighteen hours straight and see no results, but your goals will keep you properly oriented for success no matter how difficult things may seem in the moment.

The things that we can call "goals" can be divided into two groups, business goals and personal goals. At first glance it seems there's not much to separate the two, but in reality there is. It is often our personal goals that give us reasons to set business goals, just as it is our business goals that will put us on the path to the achievement of our personal goals.

It is usually easy to say which goals are business and which are personal. "I want three kids," is a personal goal, while "I want to have 15 employees by next quarter" is most certainly a business goal. However, a goal like "I want to be worth $2.5 Million by my thirtieth birthday" may be both a personal and business goal. We will call this type of goal a "critical goal," because it is something that is essential to both your personal and business goals. Critical goals are the most important type of goals, and therefore, should be the first type of goals you set.

Critical goals may include your net worth, your social status, or when you want to retire, as these things are often contingent on both business goals and personal goals. Critical goals should both be set with a comprehension of other goals you have and as starting blocks for the other goals you will make for yourself.

Begin with this simple exercise. You will need to take at least a half hour to do this, so set aside some time and jump right in (you're going to need a piece of paper and something to write with):

1.   Do you see yourself getting married? If yes, when do you want this to occur? You can't necessarily know when you will meet the person of your dreams, but it can be helpful to determine around when you might be looking for a life partner, as this may be the most important goal in life.
2.   Do you want children? If you do, how many children do you think you might want? When would you want children? Would it be shortly after you get married or several years after?
3.   When do you want to retire? Don't worry about how much money you might need to retire, because we will talk about this later. That being said, keep it realistic. Even if you made millions of dollars tomorrow you would likely still have to work for several years before you can be certain that you are financially secure for retirement.

These three things are important to understanding the bigger picture goals that you have, both personally and financially. For example, children are very expensive and you'll need to factor that kind of thing into the picture when you are setting other goals. Retiring too early can be risky, especially if you run out of money when you are at an advanced age. You also don't want to work at an unsatisfactory job any longer than you need to. With these three goals laid out, you can begin to form a clearer picture of the life you want to live down the road.

Notice how the three goals above are immaterial. These intangible goals are what provide the skeleton for the other material goals to build up. Now we can begin to see the other things that you would like to have down the road. Knowing that you want to retire at fifty opens up other paths for goals to be set.

- How much traveling do you want to do? Would you prefer to travel only when you retire, or would you rather slow your career down now and travel as much as you can before all the great sites are gone?
- Would you like to own vacation homes, or would you rather not be tethered to specific locations for travel? Perhaps you wouldn't even own a permanent home, but instead be constantly traveling the world, never knowing where you'll end up next?
- Do you have any hobbies that you may want to take up when you retire? How expensive are these hobbies? How much time would it take to learn these hobbies? Will you take a class on woodworking or painting, or would you teach yourself these things?
- What kind of lifestyle do you want to have when you retire? Do you want to comfortably live in a nice

home, spending your days walking around town, going to shops and local concerts, or would you rather live on the road, traveling constantly, visiting museums in distant countries and hiking some of the world's great peaks?

Of course this list isn't entirely comprehensive, but it should give you a clear understanding of what your retirement should look, which in turn, will help you orient your more immediate goals. If you want to travel a lot when you retire then you may not have to do much traveling now, instead focusing on your career and building your wealth. But if you feel you must travel now, then you might have to rethink your retirement age to fit in better with your goals now. This isn't to say you can't generate a sizable income on the road, in fact many of the things that will be taught in this book will show you how to make any amount of money from anywhere with an internet connection, but it is still important to consider all factors when setting goals.

Now that we have a clearer picture of what your retirement should look like, we need to set more immediate goals. These goals are things that you want to accomplish soon. These goals might be marriage, raising a family, building your business, or simply eating healthy.

We are working within a framework here that places the emphasis on your retirement, as this is often something that people look forward to in their life. Feel free to tweak this framework and place the emphasis on other things if you want, but to most people, at least, retirement serves as good a starting point.

You should now create a timeline on your piece of paper. At the end of it should be your retirement. Write down at least five immediate goals you would like to accomplish within the next five years.

When you are finished with your timeline, you should note how many of your five-year goals are personal and how many are business. If the personal goals outweigh the business goals, you may have to consider that as a potential obstacle for your business goals, just as business goals may conflict with some of your personal goals. That being said, it's up to you to decide which are more important, and need more attention.

In the example above, I included that I want to both buy a house and make $1.5 Million. If I want $1.5 Million in liquid assets, this would essentially mean that I would have to make $1.5 Million plus the value of the house I want to buy. It is certainly doable, in fact it is more than doable, anyone can both make $1.5 Million and buy a house within five years, but you have to consider the full value of that when you eventually begin thinking about how your business should operate. A business that makes $1.5 Million or more in five years is relatively easy to construct, but you still have to factor all of this in from the start.

Now that you have the major goals written down you can now start listing every other goal you might have. Take the next fifteen minutes and just see what you come up with. Some advice I have is to keep a notebook handy wherever you go for the next few weeks (you can use your phone notebook if you want) and whenever you think of something that resembles a goal you have, write it down in the notebook. Within a couple of weeks, you should have at least twenty written down that will give you a very clear picture of how you want your life to be in the near or distant future. Everyone's goals are different, which is why we aren't going to spend much more time discussing this, but as you will soon come to understand, the goals we set now will have a very positive impact on our success in the future.

Setting goals allows us to clearly interpret the defining parts of our character. Our character changes for the better when we can fully appreciate what it means to be ourselves. One person may be very interested in history and want to write a book of his own on a particularly interesting subject for him, another may want to become a famous pianist and be renowned for her musical talents, while still another may simply want to live a life of comfort, where she spends her days in leisure on a beautiful estate, planting flowers and riding horses for pleasure. Whatever your goals may be, it is greatly important that everyone develop an extensive list of those things he or she wants to achieve in life, because without such a list, none of us can be guided down the right path and make decisions with great clarity of direction in the hopes of leading ourselves down that right path.

Chapter Two:
Commitment

Now that you have developed your goals and have laid out a clear understanding of the future you want to have for yourself, you must now focus on the immediate steps you will take in pursuing your goals. You must commit to success. We can all yearn for success, spending hours each day dreaming about our goals and the future we would like to lead, but if we do not commit to the achievement of that future we will never find success.

As we have made clear, success is being able to achieve every single goal you have in life. You can only call yourself successful when you have at your disposal the tools with which you can fulfill all the goals you have ever set for yourself. Do not misunderstand the last chapter's message and attempt to pursue each goal individually. Instead, you need to orient your life around the pursuit of all the goals collectively. Think of your goals as all being in a lockbox.

You cannot pursue your goal of owning a sports car if you do not also pursue your goal of owning a beach house, or studying music, or getting married. These goals are all interwoven to form the tapestry of success that will define your character as a prosperous human being. It is only after you have found success that you will be given the keys to the lockbox of your goals.

When you work on your business, on your health, or on your social status, you should not be working to fulfillment of singular goals, but rather the fulfillment of every aspect of your dreams.

Say, for example, that you plan to lose twenty pounds in the next six months. This is a great plan to have, but don't only do this to lose twenty pounds, but do this to get yourself one step closer to success, to the fulfillment of every single goal you have. When you lose twenty pounds you become healthier, and the healthier you are the more you will be able to work on your business, the more attractive you will be to potential partners, and all of this inches you closer and closer to success.

The purpose of this book so far has been to orient yourself towards success. Now that we understand that success is not one thing but, rather, many goals, it is now much easier to work towards success. I mentioned earlier that we can all yearn for success, but few people ever achieve it. This is because those people fail to do what we have already done, which is to consolidate all of their goals into the unified goal of success. We can use the image of a beach house or a sports car as a visual reminder of our goals, but you must remember that you are not simply working for that beach house, but for the total achievement of success.

Success is what you should see when you picture your future, not just a sports car and a private jet. Success is now the only thing you should be focused on in life, because success means being able to achieve every one of your goals.

Now that we are oriented towards success and not some poorly constructed jumble of goals in your head, we can now learn to commit to success. You will not be successful until you completely commit to it. If our lives are cluttered with other commitments then we will be incapable of finding success, because our energy will be stretched too thin. Don't try balancing school, work, and entrepreneurship together, it won't work. Instead completely surrender yourself to your entrepreneurship if you think that will make you successful.

It is important to note that not everyone will be successful in life. For some of us it will be far too risky to drop everything else and focus on success. Do not do this if you cannot afford the risk. If you found that your personal goals conflict too much with your business goals, then you may have to settle for one or the other. The pursuit of success is a dangerous road to follow. It can lead to alienation from friends and family, it can lead to bankruptcy and the loss of life savings, and it can lead to great struggle and pain. But the pursuit of success can also lead to great things, like finding love, raising a prosperous family, becoming famous, helping others, and so many other wonderful things in life. All you must know is that there are risks involved, and if you can't take those risks then success may not be for you.

If success is for you, however, then you have to go out and find it. Don't sit around waiting for it to simply come to you; get up and create success for yourself. Success isn't something that is given to some, it is something that is generated by people by themselves. Do not think that because you grew up in a low-income household that you will never find success, for all you need to be successful is the willfulness to create it.

You have already taken the first step towards the creation of success. By reading this book you will come to learn more about the potential channels through which you can find success online. Online success especially has great potential for those who may not have much money to start out, as many of the things discussed in this book are relatively inexpensive and provide great starting blocks for the development of success. Be warned, though, that you will not be successful by simply reading a book or two. You have to completely immerse yourself in the entrepreneurial world, first by reading books and articles online. Then you must study the aspects of the niche markets you find promising, possibly finding a mentor or an online course that will help guide you as you take your first steps in the world of entrepreneurship. You need to make mistakes, so that you can learn hands-on what works and what doesn't in the business world. You have to work hard, often for hours on end and possibly missing out on other things that stand in the way of your success. And there are many other things you will have to do in order to learn to be successful, but it is important to realize that these things, as challenging as some of them may be, are essential to developing the skills that will lead you on the path to success.

This leads us to the point of this chapter, which is to make a commitment to success. This commitment means simply getting into the mindset of working hard and always reaching closer and closer to success. Commitment is a state-of-mind. It works within our heart to constantly propel ourselves further and further down the road towards success. It means not just yearning for your goals, but acting on the things you learn about business and entrepreneurship. It's about attention to detail, and not being satisfied until you think what you've done is the best you can do.

Notice how many times I have used the word success so far in the last chapter and a half. By my own count, I have used it over sixty times so far, and this is not an accident. I am trying to nudge you towards success, making you fixate on it so that you might realize just how important it is. From this point forward, success should be what drives every action you make. Do not be misguided by the sensation of immediate gratification, for this will weaken your mind and prevent you from achieving success. Instead of watching your favorite T.V. show for the eleventh time, commit to working hard. You can build up to this by taking one hour out of every day this week and spend that time working on your business. Next week take two hours every day to do this, and the week after that take three hours. After several weeks you will have come to work as long a time for your success as you could possibly work. These work hours, at first, may seem tedious and unfulfilling, but as you continue working every day and develop ideas and plans for your business you will likely find that you don't have enough time for all the work you want to do every day.

Commitment is ideally done all the way. The greatest chances of success will be found when you completely immerse yourself in your work from the start, but the exercise above can be helpful in showing you what commitment means and how beneficial it can be for your pursuit of success.

Keep in mind though, that this process won't be easy. In the beginning you'll enjoy the new work, but after a while you'll start to get disillusioned. You might be working long hours, and not seeing any results. However, if you really want to be successful, you have to persevere, because if you don't, you have no chance for success. I want to make it clear to you that success is not something that you stumble upon through chance, rather it is something that can always be created by you. Some will have to struggle more than others to create it, but there is always the opportunity for success when you work hard enough for it. Those individuals who do not find success in life simply haven't worked hard enough for it, but once you understand this truth and fully embrace it, then nothing can stop you from finding success. You are the only thing that stands in your way of success, and only when you allow yourself to be successful will you finally be successful.

Most importantly, you have to convince yourself that you will be successful. Working hard while believing in your own success is hard, but working hard while not believing in yourself is impossible. In that sense, your own beliefs on success become self-fulfilling.

You must make the decision to commit as soon as possible. Once you truly commit to success, you will find yourself completely immersed inside the realm of success. It is essential to know that this is something you genuinely want. As I've said before, success is not for everyone, and that is perfectly fine. There is nothing stopping you from living a life of relative comfort and simplicity, but if you truly want to live the most successfully you can, then you must be willing to make sacrifices and turn yourself over to the work you will be undertaking.

In terms of the work you will be doing there are many different options that will put you on the road to success. The rest of this book will focus on entrepreneurship on the internet, and we will be going in depth into the various paths you can take as an internet entrepreneur. This will become important to your commitment. When you commit to success you will begin to notice possibilities in every aspect of your life. You will be always on the lookout for new ideas and markets that you can delve into to make money. You will see the opportunities for success when you buy coffee in the morning, when you sit in traffic on the expressway, when you are out on a walk, or surfing the internet. Do not think that just because you are not actively working in these moments that there are not lessons to be learned from them. In fact, it is during these mundane tasks that many of your best ideas will be realized. Take surfing the internet for example, on the internet most of the content you will interact with has some sort of cash-flow behind it. This isn't to say that nothing on the internet is of high-quality or that it is all designed for making money, because much of what you find on the internet is very helpful and insightful, but the greatest benefit that these things may provide you with is through exposing you to the inner-workings of online business. You will begin to see patterns all around you, and these patterns will offer insight into how you might design your business for success.

This insight will provide you with the tools and knowledge to take your commitment to success to the next level. Commitment is not real unless you are willing to act on it. Soon after committing to success you will be eager to jump right in and experiment with your business ideas. Listen to your gut and dive right in and play around with those ideas. You will learn more and more about business the deeper you wade into the business realm. This is why you must continually work towards success, because every minute you spend working on your business the closer you will be to success and the sooner you will find it.

Now that you have truly committed to success you are ready to take the next step. You need to learn as much as you can to properly orient yourself for the path you will eventually want to take. You cannot know quite yet which online business path you want to take yet, because many of them only appeal to certain types of people. Those who want to see short-term financial success really quickly might be more interested in Amazon marketing, where you can quickly earn money, but those who want to create a long-term personal brand might be drawn to blogging, which offers a slower pace in the short-term but much greater payoff in the long run. You need to be informed as much as possible before you can make the decision as to which path you want to take. This is the real purpose of this book; to show you exactly which path is the best for you to take.

Do not feel, however, that you can skip over certain aspects of this book you feel don't interest you, because you must have a deep understanding of the world of online business before you begin to think about choosing a specific market. The power you might have as a blogger is very much influenced by your ability to anticipate potential partnerships and cooperation with those involved in Amazon or YouTube. If you can effectively use all of the available tools at your disposal, you have a much greater chance at success than someone who neglected to learn other markets involved in the online platform. The internet is an amazing tool for you as a businessperson, but it is very complicated and everything about it is interwoven and connected. There is great overlap between the various online mediums, and being able to not only understand those mediums, but use them to your advantage will greatly assist you in your development of a successful online business.

SECTION TWO:
Developing Your Brand on the Online Market

Chapter Three:
The Online Business Market

Generally speaking, the online business market can be split into two types of markets, freelancing and personal branding. Freelancing is when you sell your skills to people willing to pay you money for it. This can be many things, from coding, to website design, to voice acting, and countless others. Online freelancing is an enormous market, with literally millions of people selling their skills to companies and individuals willing to hire them. There is a decent amount of competition and you should really only consider this line of work if you are very good at your particular skill, like being a fantastic writer or a really good graphic designer. Personal branding, on the other hand, is slightly less competitive, not because there are fewer people doing it, but because more people can create personal brands that sell without having to have a larger customer base. The majority of this book will cover personal branding, because you, yourself, not your skills, can turn into a very profitable enterprise. We will discuss freelancing in a future chapter, though, because, as I have mentioned before, understanding the market as a whole is important to developing a strong online business, and you will most likely hire freelancers to create things for your brand and your company.

To the untrained observer, the online market is filled with a wide range of different companies and people, all doing something unique. This is, in fact, an incorrect way of viewing the internet market. Everyone online, who is successfully trying to sell you a product, has created a personal brand. They are trying to connect their product or service with you by establishing trust with you through their brand.

Let's say that you are the owner of an online beauty supply company. You sell makeup and other beauty products, but because the competition for beauty products online is fierce, you only make $2,000 a month. This is because you have not effectively created a personal brand. Effectively marketed companies use a spokesperson to establish a personal relationship with their customers. Even more effective companies target a very specific segment of the population. Don't try selling makeup to everyone, it's a way too competitive market for that. Instead, be specific. Try to sell to busy mothers, or women over sixty, or some other small demographic. This way you can claim your product to be the "makeup for busy mothers," or the "makeup for active grandmothers." If you simply try selling a product, especially online, and don't pinpoint exactly who your customer is, then you will not make money.

These are the two most important aspects of a good online business, being able to identify and relate to your customers, and defining yourself as a prominent leader within your market through personal branding. We will discuss these at length in the next chapter, but keep this in mind and you will be able to frame the online market more appropriately.

Before you can start your online business, you must come to understand exactly what makes it so useful for your business. The internet was created as a way to quickly share information with the entire world, but it survives because of its enormous potential to make people money.

Think of companies like Facebook or Amazon. These companies are two of the largest companies on the planet, Amazon itself is poised to be the first trillion-dollar company in a couple decades or sooner, but they only exist because of the internet.

These companies were created with the internet in mind, there is no doubt about that, but they did not simply use the internet to position themselves for success, they used their brand to change the internet from its simple beginnings as a place to share information into the world's largest marketplace, where billions of dollars are exchanged every day.

People now use the internet as a place to purchase goods and pay for services, and it shouldn't be too long before every transaction is made through the internet. Think about it, when you buy food at the grocery store using a credit card, the money reaches the grocery store from the internet, not from yourself. It is only when we pay in cash that we directly pay for goods and services, and even that may involve the internet to some extent.

One of the most successful internet companies, PayPal, has made a fortune by acting as middleman between consumers and producers. They charge a transaction fee for every exchange done through their website, but companies are willing to pay the transaction fee because PayPal is convenient and safe for people to use and they know that their customers value that. PayPal is so successful because it was able to change the way we pay for things.

I am not suggesting that you try to start a massive internet company that will change the internet forever, at least not yet. But you have to understand that the internet is constantly changing shape and what is important on the internet one day may be completely different within just a few months. I fully expect this book to be useless in fifteen years, because the internet will have turned into something completely different by then, and nothing I teach you in this book will be relevant anymore, except for this information here.

In order to be successful on the internet you must be adaptive to the changing environment of its marketplace. Unlike other markets, like the global business markets, or even local small-business markets, the internet does not change for obvious reasons. When international conflicts break out, we can expect that the global marketplace will be affected, but on the internet market things act differently. Seemingly small things can have a massive effect on the internet, and it is all but impossible to recognize what these things will be. Remember a few years ago, when a picture of a dress took the internet by storm, and people were asking whether the dress was colored blue and black or white and gold? This went viral, but who could have predicted such an event? The photo was an interesting phenomenon, but there are millions of interesting things on the internet that never go viral.

You can't expect to know when things will go viral and when they will change the entire face of the internet forever, but you can understand and appreciate that the internet is constantly changing and that if you are to be successful in such an environment you must be able to stay on your toes and prepare for any unforeseen changes that come your way.

The internet can be seen as an immense jungle that is filled with undiscovered creatures and landscapes that we, the explorers of such a jungle, have been tasked with traversing and civilizing. There are new and exciting discoveries to be made around every corner, and those who can quickly navigate the jungle will be able to claim as much of those discoveries as their own, and be able to market their success above others.

There are things about the internet that no one knows about or understands, but the deeper into the jungle we go, the more we will know about it, and the better prepared we will be to use its resources for our own gain.

As we have already established, the jungle market of the internet is essentially divided into two major markets, freelancing and personal branding, but within these markets exist many other smaller markets. Within the macro-market of personal branding, the micro-markets that will provide you with the greatest chances of success are the Amazon market, the YouTube market, the Blogging market, and traditional business market. We will discuss these micro-markets at length in their respective chapters, but we must look at them within the context of the macro-market of the internet first, before we can fully appreciate how useful they can be to your personal success.

Remember, again, that these three micro-markets operate under the sphere of personal branding. Every single person who has been successful on Amazon, YouTube, the Blogosphere, or on their own website has effectively used personal branding in the development of their products or content, whether they knew what they were doing or not. You will come to appreciate, during the course of the rest of this book, that personal branding is your greatest tool to put you on the path towards success and the achievement of every one of your goals. But we must learn what personal branding is before you will appreciate its power.

Personal branding, as we briefly defined at the beginning of this chapter, is being able to develop a sense of trust between you and your customer, and understanding what those customers expect from you as a producer. The most successful producers on the internet, people like PewDiePie or Casey Neistat to name a couple, are able to use their personality to their advantage in establishing trust with their customers. When they sell a product of theirs, the customers with whom they have established a trustworthy relationship won't hesitate much in purchasing products from them. This is because their customers have grown to like them as people—because they're funny, or thoughtful, or they offer a unique perspective on the world around them—not because they offer spectacular, or innovate products.

Throughout history there have been people who have used trust to sell their products. This is because trust is perhaps the single most important thing about sales and if you can't establish trust, then you won't sell anything. Think of the "Medicine Shows" that we have all seen on television programs about the Wild West. Salesmen would go from town to town trying to sell "miracle elixirs" that would supposedly cure diseases and prevent chronic pain. These salesmen wouldn't just show up at the county fair and tell people to buy their product, but would package their elixirs in quality medical bottles, claim that it has been used before to cure the diseases they claimed it did, and that the "President himself uses this product!" They would also develop a brief relationship with the people they were trying to sell to. They would ask questions about your health, your family; they might tell a few jokes to lighten the mood, and they would likely take a dose of the elixir themselves, to prove to you that *you* needed to use their product.

I am certainly not advocating telling lies about your product to sell it. In fact, this probably wouldn't even work; have you ever heard of a millionaire elixir salesman? But what I am advocating is developing a relationship with your customers. A business that is cold and unwelcoming to their customers has practically no chance of success on the internet or elsewhere. A successful internet businessperson will genuinely care about their customers and will consequently be able to develop an even more trusting relationship with their customers that will lead to even more sales.

You are unlikely to succeed on the internet if you only care about making the money, because your customers will be able to sense this, even through all the smoke and mirrors that you may have set up. Don't attempt to rip people off, don't lie or cheat, and don't be selfish. Just understand that you are dependent on your customers far more than they are dependent on you.

On the internet you have literally billions of potential customers but you also have a massive amount of competition. It is essential, therefore, to find your niche so that you can effectively relate to your customers and hopefully develop a close circle of customers who consistently return to you to buy your products. A niche is like a special segment of the market that is carved out just for you. It allows you to focus your attention on a part of the market that has not been over-sold yet. Finding a niche in which you can operate with relative exclusivity will allow you to sell as many products as you can.

One of the lessons I have learned in developing several internet businesses, is that it is better to sell more products to fewer people than it is to sell fewer products to more people. I cannot stress this enough. Do not think that you can sell your product once, to a million people. Instead think that you can sell your product one hundred times, to ten-thousand. The mathematical results of both of these situations are the same, but you cannot realistically expect to reach one million people with your brand, even by harnessing the power of the internet, but you can very easily reach ten-thousand people and sell them a good product many times over.

Using the example of a beauty product store again, let's say that you market yourself to busy mothers, and you sell a palette of makeup for $20. Because your customer base is small and the number of people you need to market to is fewer, you can build a more personal relationship with each of your customers, effectively increasing your chances of success. The market research you have done for your business suggests that the average busy mother will buy one of these palettes every month, which means every customer who buys on a regular basis from your company will spend $240 every year. If you do the math, you would only need to have fewer than 5,000 customers a year to make more than a million dollars.

See how the development of a strong customer base is so important? All you need are a few thousand customers and your business can make well over one million dollars every year. Not to mention that when you develop personal relationships with your customers they will buy from you on a regular basis, providing you with consistent income for the foreseeable future.

We will cover this topic in depth in future chapters but you need to keep in mind how important it is to develop relationships with your customers.

The beauty of the internet is that there is so much available that no one person or company can dominate the whole market. Amazon does a pretty good job of covering most of the industries on the internet, but what you will come to learn in the chapter on the Amazon market is that Amazon doesn't really produce any of their products, but they act as a middleman between the businesses that produce their products and sell it to their customers. You can buy anything from a new pair of shoes to beauty supplies to food on Amazon, but you aren't necessarily buying them directly from Amazon, you are merely buying these products through Amazon from another business. You, as an online businessperson can use Amazon to sell your products, and we will discuss this in a future chapter, but remember that Amazon does not dominate the market of production, and you can very easily use Amazon to develop your personal brand of products and further your online business.

Because the internet services billions of people every day, your chances of success as an online businessperson are as numerous as you can imagine. The trick to success online is in finding your niche, and then developing your personal brand within that niche so that you can sell as many of your products as you can, and we will discuss this in the markets section of this book. But before we can learn which niches to sell in, we have to learn a little bit more about the development of your personal brand and the relationships you need to build with your customers.

Chapter Four:
Developing a Personal Brand

Personal brands act to unite you as a person with the products or services you are selling through your business. When people think about the clothes you are selling, the courses you offer, or the posters you make they should be thinking about you.

You can look at your products and services in relationship to your personal brand as the relationship between an artist and his artwork. Take an artist like Pablo Picasso, who is seen through the artwork he produced. When someone looks at a painting or sculpture of his, they see his personal style reflected in each stroke of the brush and every groove of the clay. You wouldn't look at one of his paintings and say "This is my favorite painting by this artist," instead you would say "This is my favorite *Picasso*." You would immediately identify Picasso as the artist, and see the painting as a reflection of him as a person, more than that.

In fact, you see Pablo Picasso and his painting as one and the same. The same should be true in your personal brand. You and your brand should be one and the same.

This goes back to what I said in the second chapter about commitment. By the time you produce your brand you will have completely immersed yourself in your work, and this should be evident to anyone interested in purchasing the product or service you offer.

If you sell iPhone cases, for example, your own personal touch should be seen in the case itself, not just on the website you sell them through, or the Facebook page dedicated to your brand. It is this uniqueness of both marketing and product that gives you an edge as an online businessperson. When you try to sell something to someone, especially in such a competitive market, you must present your case as to why your product is unique, and why customers should pick your product over a competitor's. When you and the product you are selling are the same thing, when you are, in essence, selling yourself, you will find the greatest success in your business.

In order to establish a personal brand, you must define your unique qualities as a human being and a businessperson and use those qualities to develop your brand.

What makes you a unique person? Do you have a specific skill or interest that sets you apart from most people?

Once you can identify certain qualities about yourself that are unique you can use those qualities to generate a product or service that fits in line with your unique attributes. Unique products are often the ones that sell the most.

You can learn a lot from celebrities who have accentuated a particular quality and used that to gain fame. Lady Gaga, for example, derives much of her popularity from her often strange looking costumes. Her music is certainly unique, but her attire is what always draws attention, and this creates an air of mystery surrounding her as a person that interests people and helps sells her music.

There are two important points in the last paragraph that are extremely important to the development of a personal brand. These are that you shouldn't stray too far from the mainstream, but you should also draw attention to yourself. That is, you must strike a balance between being unorthodox and gaining the right amount of attention. If you're too orthodox with your brand, people will think you're boring and you don't offer anything new for them. If you're too unorthodox, people will think you are strange and will be discouraged from buying from you. If you are just the right amount of unorthodox, people will like you and think you are interesting, which in turn will enable you to build a personal brand.

Lady Gaga does a fantastic job of floating right on the edge of the "mainstream" with her brand. She sometimes dresses in shocking attire, but she never strays too far, and she never crosses any lines.

The lesson to be learned here is one of conventional unorthodoxy. Capitalize on what has been deemed to be an acceptable amount of uniqueness.

The other point I want to make is that you must draw attention to yourself with your brand. There may seem to be a contradiction between what I've said about not straying far from the mainstream and drawing attention to yourself, but let me assure you, there is no contradiction. You must create unique qualities, in line with what is acceptable, and infuse those qualities within your brand.

These unique qualities set you apart from the competition and draw attention to your brand. You need to have something flashy but not too daring.

This uniqueness can be fulfilled by the set of skills you defined earlier in this chapter, but make sure they can draw people's attention sufficiently, or else you won't be able to successfully market your brand.

Your unique qualities will act as the starting block for the way in which you will market your brand. Marketing should not be seen as a separate function, but rather something that is naturally accomplished by a properly constructed brand.

A brand that will be successful is one that can organically market itself to a certain extent. The better your brand can ride the line of conventional unorthodoxy then the more efficiently you will be at marketing your brand. This is because of the aspect of attention grabbing that is essential to the brand you are creating; with a unique brand comes attention, and with attention comes marketing.

As we learned in the last chapter, the internet is very competitive. The greatest tool that you can use to beat the competition is your personal brand. You must make it better, more affordable, and more available to people than your competitor's brand. Good products will sell themselves. If you have put enough effort into the development of your brand and have used this book to find a niche that works for you, then your brand will often times create its own success.

The relationship between your brand and its marketing is not always symbiotic, and that isn't always your fault, sometimes your brand is just not meant to generate its own success. While we will spend time discussing specific marketing techniques in future chapters, I want to lay the foundation for the basics of online marketing practices that will better position your business for success.

Gone are the days of the newspaper ads, the paper letter campaigns, and giant billboards on the side of highways. These types of marketing campaigns were able to reach many people, but are all but obsolete in the age of the internet, when platforms like Facebook, Instagram, and YouTube dominate the advertising industry and are able to reach even more people with a single marketing campaign.

These massive companies are your friend when it comes to marketing your brand. Although upfront costs for advertising on their interface may seem steep, they are often relatively low compared to alternative media, and they most certainly reach a larger audience than other types of advertising, especially print. They're also very precise, and you can often set parameters for who you want to see your ads.

Of course, print advertising should not be completely discounted, even for an online business. Print is still a preferred method for many, and they do still publish newspapers every day, so depending on who is part of your customer base, you may need to consider print advertising as a potentially useful tool. Just remember that as an online business you must focus your available resources on the type of marketing you think will be most effective for the brand you are trying to sell. You should only use print media if you're sure that they are going to be effective for your brand, and successfully target the people in your niche.

Pinpointing the type of marketing that will be most successful at spreading the word about brand is essential to the success of your business. Remember that the best developed brands will market themselves, but to use your brand's built-in propensities you must use your resources to their greatest effect. This is true of less than perfect brands as well, because marketing will become the single most important aspect of the brand you are about to build.

An effective set of marketing campaigns can mean all the difference to your company, both in the short-term and the long-term. The greater number of people you can reach, and the more effective your marketing is on that population, the greater chances that your brand has for success. Essentially, the two greatest aspects of marketing your brand will be population size and the effectiveness of your advertisement.

You will find a continuing discussion on these two aspects of marketing campaigns in the next section of this book. For the time being, however, you must know that the step that naturally follows the development of your brand is the marketing of that brand to your customers.

Chapter Five:
Working with Your Customers

In the last chapter we talked about how you can develop a successful brand. We learned about unifying yourself with your brand, the principle of conventional unorthodoxy, and the importance of marketing your brand to your customers.

It is this last point that acts as a good bridge between this chapter and the last one, because the creation of an effective marketing campaign is contingent on your understanding of your customers.

To properly know who your customers are and what they are likely to want from you, your brand, the types of products/services you sell, and to find out the best kind of marketing campaign you can do, you need to ask various questions about the nature of the customers you are trying to sell to.

Most of these questions are of a demographic nature: What gender are most of your customers? What age are most of your customers? What economic class are you most likely to target? Is there a specific niche that these people follow that you might be able to target?

Some of these questions are more focused on your brand in relation to your customer's population: How much of the population listed above will you attempt to reach with your brand? Are there certain subsets of this population with whom your brand will not be well received? Are there aspects of your brand that you may need to accentuate in order to properly draw attention from this population?

This is by no means a complete list of questions, as often the questions you must ask about your customers will be specific to the types of people your customers are and the nature of your brand, but this should give you an idea of the kinds of questions you should ask yourself in order to better understand your customers and appreciate what they might mean for your success.

Naturally, your greatest customer relationships will be built with people with whom you have a lot in common. For example, if your brand revolves around football, then you will probably have more in common with sports fans than other parts of the population, and therefore you can establish strong relationships with those sports fans solely based off of the nature of your brand. This goes back to what we talked about in the last chapter about uniting yourself with your brand. If you and your brand are one, and you, when you are selling your products or services, are essentially selling yourself, then it is monumentally important that you like the kind of product your brand offers. If you don't really like sports all that much, then you shouldn't think about creating your business around football.

This is why it is so important that you spend the time to really learn about the online business market. If you don't fully appreciate all of its intricacies you may choose the wrong niche to build you brand in and you will, in turn, be disadvantaged by this.

Building relationships with your customers seems like an obvious step to the development of a successful business, but you may not be able to build those relationships if you do not choose the appropriate field for yourself. Pick a market that you are passionate about, and pick a niche that satisfies that passion.

When you take the time to find the right sub-market for your brand you will find it to be so much easier to establish lasting relationships with your customers.

That brings me to the next point I want to make about your relationship with your customers. Your customers are not expendable. You do not use your customers, they use you. You depend on your customers.

You are completely and totally dependent on your customers for success. If you have no customers, you will make no money; it's as simple as that. Because of this you must do your best to establish lasting relationships. The unfortunate reality of business is that many businessmen believe that their customers are a tool which they can use to make money. It is, in fact, the other way around. You, and your business, are the ones being used to buy a product or service that someone wants. You put your brand out there because you feel that there is something to be gained from selling it, but your brand is still being used for some purpose by someone other than yourself.

Perhaps even more important than realizing how indispensable your customers are, is understanding that if you cannot be sure that your existing customers return on a regular basis then you will likewise not be successful.

Once you have grown your online business to an acceptable size and gathered a respectable number of customers, your objectives should be refocused on keeping your existing customers. It costs less to retain customers, and they will buy more from you than any prospective customers will.

The most successful companies, both online and not, are often successful because of their loyal customer base, not necessarily because their products are especially good or they offer their products at a lower cost, but because they have treated their customers well and have attempted to know their customers like friends.

Do not treat your customers like tools and you will be able to gain their favor over other companies who may even offer superior products at better prices. Customers are people, and people don't appreciate it when they are thrown around by big businesses that do not care about their needs. If you can prove that your company does care about your customers, then you are more likely to gain loyal customers who will continue returning to you to buy from.

Big companies find success because they dominate the market and offer cheaper prices for things. Your advantage over big companies is, in fact, your small size. This affords you the time to get to know your customers in a way that bigger companies cannot, and will in turn give you a leg up when customers make the decision as to which business to buy from.

Other ways to ensure that your customers remain loyal to your brand include creating an email list, offering discounts to returning customers, and offering exclusive content to people who have subscribed.

The basic idea behind an email list is creating a directory of people who are interested in your brand. This can be done by asking people to give their email when they first check out your website and by connecting that email to a marketing service. These marketing services make it very easy to collect customer's emails and including those emails in an email campaign that you launch. This way you can directly reach customers who have shown their interest in your brand by actively visiting your website and joining the email list. You waste less money on advertising, and thus increase retention rates, when you target people you know have a higher likelihood of buying from you.

While it is important to reach out to other people through Facebook, or Instagram, or some other platform, it is equally important that you focus on the people who have already interacted in some way with your brand.

To keep customers interested in your product you can offer discounts for products or services you offer. Let's say that you sell a collection of eBooks through your blog. These eBooks are typically priced for $5 apiece and you sell one eBook to 1,000 people, meaning you collect $5,000 earnings from the eBooks without even telling your previous customers about the eBook. One month later you come out with a new eBook. You sell this one for the exact same price and generate the exact same number of organic customers, but this time you offer a sale for 10% off to all the 1,000 people who bought from you the month before. Your customers receive an email offer and one-quarter of those people buy your eBook. This means that you make an extra $1,125 just by telling your old customers about your new eBook and by offering a discount. Not only do you make more than one-thousand dollars from this email campaign, but you also expose your returning customers to even more of your products and likely gain a few more loyal customers who like the products you sell.

It may seem foolish to offer products at discounted rates, but exposing customers to more of your brand is essential to keep customers loyal to you. The more exposed to your brand the customers are, then the more likely they are to care about your products and return to you for their future purchases.

Again I must stress the importance of your presence in your personal brand. Your success online is contingent on your ability to create a marketable personal brand. This brand is only marketable to your customers if you promote yourself as a trustworthy, caring, and interesting person. Because of the competition online it is essential that you stress the qualities that make you unique in order to develop relationships with your customers.

Your customers will return to your brand because they like you. It is essential to understand when developing your personal brand that your customers are initially drawn to your brand because of the product or service you offer them, but they return because they find you, as the representative of your personal brand, to be better than others who are offering similar products.

The success of your personal brand will depend on how well you can establish relationships with your customers so that they will return to your brand and buy from you.

It is because of this that you must learn who your customers are. Ask them questions, respond to emails and messages they send you, and involve them in your brand. If you do these things you will learn more about your customers than you could possibly do otherwise.

Your online business should be focused on a particular segment of the population for this very reason. You will be incapable of communicating with your customers and developing relationships with them if your brand covers too wide a market.

This is why you must narrowly focus your brand on particular markets, and within those markets you must locate sub-markets that serve even fewer people. I mentioned in the beginning of this book how there are three markets in which you will find the greatest amount of success for your business and your personal brand, and within these three markets exist many smaller markets that may fit your unique qualities perfectly and allow you to generate a solid customer base whom you can rely on for a dependable income.

Knowing what you know after reading the first two sections of this book, you need to return to the list of goals you wrote down in chapter one and consider them in light of what you have learned in the past few chapters. Is there anything you need to change? Anything you want to add?

In the next section of this book we will delve deeply into the three main markets contained within the internet and learn how you can develop a personal brand that fits nicely into one of these markets.

Your customers, whether on YouTube, Amazon, or on your Blog, will appreciate the relationship you build with them through your brand, but you must keep your goals in the back of your head at all times and frame your personal brand in terms of those goals.

SECTION THREE:
Markets

Chapter Six:
The Amazon Market

The Amazon market departs slightly from the rule of personal branding that we have spent the last section of this book discussing. This is not to say that personal brands have no place on Amazon, because you can use your personal brand to sell products on Amazon and you will always want to include your own logo on the products you sell, but Amazon isn't the best place to try and develop your personal brand, although it can be a good place to test your online business skills.

Amazon is often one of the first places that people look to when they consider starting an online business. As Amazon is poised to be the first trillion-dollar company, they have the resources to help you sell products and make good money doing so. There are many people who make thousands of dollars a day selling their products on

Amazon, and there are some who make even more than that.

These individuals have taken the time to really learn the ins and outs of the Amazon marketplace so that they can use each of the tools available on Amazon to make their business successful.

Amazon offers a program they call "Fulfillment by Amazon," or "FBA" for short. Through FBA, Amazon will store any products you sell through Amazon at one of their distribution centers for a small fee. When one of your products is sold through Amazon they will ship your product using Amazon Prime and you make money from this.

Individuals frequently sell products that they have purchased in bulk from another company at a discounted price, such as Alibaba. For example, they might buy one-thousand stuffed animals from Alibaba for 75 cents, costing them $750. They then sell the stuffed animal for $10 through Amazon, making a profit of around $6 per stuffed animal after all the fees, making a total profit of over $5,000 once they sell all of the stuffed animals.

The basic idea is very simple; you simply act as a middleman between a major production company, such as Alibaba, and Amazon and its customers. There are many things about this business, though, that become very complicated to understand.

There are hundreds of thousands of people who use FBA to make money, making the Amazon market very competitive. If you know what you're doing and you choose to sell a product in an unsaturated niche then you will likely be successful, but if not you will find it difficult to sell your products, because others will be selling similar products at even better prices.

There are many resources online that will give you specifics on how to properly set up your Amazon business for success, showing you which types of products sell the best, basic price ranges that are most successful, how many reviews you need, advice on marketing, and other important things to understand. Because of this, I will not spend an excessive amount of time giving you specifics on how to sell on Amazon, but rather help to place the Amazon marketplace within a framework for success.

Amazon FBA can be somewhat time consuming, as the research involved in finding products to sell can often take days or weeks, even with special software designed to help you find those products. You will then have to invest money into buying products in bulk and storing them in an Amazon center, then you will need to invest time and money into getting reviews written for your products and properly marketing your brand.

Remember, however, that all of the money you spend on Amazon FBA upfront is working as an investment towards future sales of your products to customers on Amazon. You will need to spend some time researching the Amazon FBA marketplace further and learn how much initial investment will be necessary before you can make money on Amazon ($1,000 is often a good starting point).

If the money that you initially invest pays off, you will be able to reinvest the money you make from sales into further establishing your products on the Amazon marketplace. This is done by branding your products.

Branding your products on Amazon will allow you to establish a solid customer base and sell further products on Amazon. Many bulk distributors like Alibaba allow you to personalize your products for a small fee, meaning that you can include a logo on the products you sell. You can use this logo to develop a brand through which you will be able to sell more products to more customers. Your customers will return to your brand over other's because they trust you; they know that the products you sell are of acceptable quality and that you can get the products to them within a reasonable time frame.

It is essential to understand that you will not be able to establish a trustworthy brand on Amazon if you do not choose the right products. This doesn't only mean finding a personal niche or an unsaturated micro-market, but also finding a product of good quality that isn't cheaply produced and doesn't break within a few days.

Do not be tempted to purchase the cheapest product you can find simply because it is the least expensive item available, because sometimes those products will be of very low quality. Although you want to find products that will cost you less, you must maintain certain standards for your products to keep your customers interested.

Find products that have low competition and high purchase rates. This isn't necessarily something that is very easy to find when you are just starting out, but once you get a feel for the market and learn more about products, prices, and competition you should be able to make educated investments into products that will make you money. If you find a product that has been sold many times without having too many people selling the same thing this is probably something you should consider investing in. There is a lot of software that can be purchased online that will help you find products that work well, but it's important that you understand what the software will be doing, so you should do this yourself when you are just starting out.

You need to communicate any questions you have about the products you're interested in with the company that manufactures those products. If you want to sell a special type of camera, then you need to know that the camera is going to work well enough to sell to your customers (this is just an example, you probably shouldn't sell cameras as there's too much competition). You can find out about the quality of certain products by speaking to someone from the manufacturing company, by researching the company and finding other products they have sold, or by simply ordering a sample of the product, as most companies will gladly send you one.

As we learned in the last chapter, it is essential that your customers trust you and the products you sell. When you create a brand on Amazon you will be responsible for any problems associated with the products you sell, even if you never see those products in person. You will find it impossible to establish trust with your customers if the products you sell are of inferior quality, and while you may be able to sell a few of those products, you will soon face bad reviews from disappointed customers that will make you lose money.

Take the time to find quality products and sell as many of those products as you can. Remember what we learned about our customers from the previous chapters, and recognize that with quality products comes satisfied customers and satisfied customers will return to your brand for any future purchases they might make.

Amazon is a wonderful starting place for your online success, and although it will require a sizable investment to start with, it is possible that it will bring you great success. Remember that the greatest success that you will find online will come after you have established a reputable brand, and Amazon can be a good place to start your brand. From there, you can expand your brand into other marketplaces, as we will discuss in the following chapters. Even if you have no interest at all in using FBA as an online business tool, it is likely that you will use Amazon in some way for your business and personal brand, so it is still necessary to know how Amazon operates and what is involved in such a successful market.

Chapter Seven:
The YouTube Market

Returning to the lessons we have learned about personal branding, the YouTube market offers the best portal through which you can develop your personal brand. Both YouTube and Blogging are dependent on a strong personal brand for success, but YouTube will allow you to develop your brand in a shorter time period than Blogging may give you. Blogging has its advantages over YouTube for sure, but YouTube is an incredibly useful tool for anyone trying to develop their personal brand within a short period of time.

It is certainly possible to develop one's personal brand on YouTube within a matter of weeks. If you log in to YouTube right now you are certain to find several channels with 100k+ subscriptions and millions of views that have only been up for a few weeks. These ultra-successful channels have all followed a plan in the development of their videos. They have learned what has made others successful on YouTube and developed their brand around that.

When developing your own channel on YouTube you need to use the following protocol to ensure that your customers return to your brand.

The YouTube Protocol:

1. Produce high quality videos
2. Tell a story
3. Give people good information
4. Upload daily
5. Have a website, Facebook, Twitter, Instagram
6. Hold livestreams or include personal vlogs
7. Maintain trust with your viewers

You must keep these seven things in mind if you decide to use YouTube to create your brand. The most important part of a successful YouTube channel is quality, and you should never waste resources on a poorly produced video. This isn't to say that videos must be Hollywood quality, it simply means that they are well constructed and deliver their message effectively. This is doubly important when you incorporate your brand into the mix, for the more effective a video is the better it will market your brand.

Successful YouTube videos are those which both provide the viewer with useful information and entertain the viewer. Storytelling will be a good way to make information-packed videos more enjoyable, just as including more information into a purely entertaining video might make the video more interesting.

If you are serious about making money on YouTube, then you should consider uploading every day. Maybe the nature of your brand makes this difficult, but you should really try to upload videos as often as possible. The more frequently you upload, the more people will be exposed to your brand in a shorter period of time, which effectively hastens the time it takes to be successful. You'll also engage your audience better, and keep old subscribers returning.

As your YouTube page will serve as the center of your brand and be connected directly to it, you should increase your internet presence as much as possible by having a website, a Facebook page, a Twitter, and an Instagram, or any other social media you might need. You should maintain a consistent presence on these sites so as to maintain your audience.

In order to maintain such a strong audience, it may also be useful to do occasional livestreams for your viewers which will allow them time to ask you questions and have their voices heard. This will make them feel like they know you personally, as you will be directly answering their questions and communicating with your viewers in a more intimate way.

All of the things described above are done in the interest of maintaining a loyal audience and developing trust. The better the content you produce and the more personable you are with your viewers the more your viewers will come to your brand instead of another brand. People will initially come to your brand out of interest for whatever topics or information you cover, but they will return because they find you trustworthy, entertaining, and, essentially, better than others who offer a similar channel.

Using YouTube to develop your brand is one of the easiest ways to market your brand and sell your products or services. YouTube is often seen as an entertainment website, but it is so much more than that. It can be used for educational purposes, technical purposes, or for simple entertainment, but in terms of its uses as a business platform, YouTube offers one of the best ways to develop your business.

Think of how much information you are bombarded with on YouTube every time you go on their website. From the videos, to the ads, to the comments, to the information in the description box, everything on YouTube is designed to provide the viewer with as much information as possible. This is what makes YouTube one of the greatest examples of the power of the internet as well as an excellent tool for anyone getting involved in the business world.

But how do you harness YouTube as a tool for your personal brand? Firstly, you should spend time watching a variety of YouTube videos, recognizing which videos make it to the "trending" list, which videos get over one million views, how many advertisements play on some videos, which videos get more likes than other, and which videos get the most comments. Try to spot the patterns in these. Although it may be hard at first, you'll come to recognize patterns that you can use for your own YouTube channel.

In order to really appreciate YouTube's business capabilities, you need to spend as much time as you can exploring the variety of videos that are uploaded to the site and study those videos to see what makes popular videos so successful. The most successful businesses that use YouTube to market their brand will upload regularly, make YouTube an extension of their website, and include links to their website, Facebook page, and anything else their selling in the description box beneath their videos.

Once you begin to realize how the YouTube business market operates you can start developing your business in terms of the YouTube platform. You should consider using YouTube as the foundation of your company, where all the material you want to communicate to your customers can be quickly delivered with ease.

People enjoy watching videos, especially if those videos are entertaining, and you should use videos to your advantage in developing and selling your personal brand.

When you begin producing your videos make sure to follow the protocol I laid out earlier in this chapter and do not forget to tailor your video to fit the customers you want to attract.

Once you initially attract your customers you can begin guiding them to your brand and the products or services you are selling.

Remember what I have said earlier about drawing people in with information and retaining them through your persona. Provide your customers with solid information about things that are relevant to your niche, but keep them coming back through the trust you build with them.

This is why I suggest that you include yourself in your videos. It is relatively easy to produce what are called "Clickbait" videos that intend on drawing in viewers quickly, usually through some sort of shock-factor or humor. While these videos can easily gain millions of views within a few weeks, it is very difficult for these videos to direct their viewers to their brand or any external website outside of YouTube. When you show yourself in your videos, however, you establish a personal relationship with your viewers in a way that is impossible to do any other way.

When you open yourself up to your viewers they already trust you more than they would otherwise. This goes back to the chapter on customers. You learned in that chapter how important the establishment of trust can be, especially in an online setting, and you must remember this lesson when you produce your videos.

Do not get me wrong, though. You can be successful without ever showing your face in your videos, but personal experience has taught me that you can find more success in a shorter period of time by including yourself in the videos you produce.

Some of the most popular videos on YouTube are "vlogs," which are longer videos that show a regular person going throughout their day. These videos give an often very intimate perspective on the life of the person behind the video and frequently allow the individual in the video to develop uniquely personal relationships with his or her audience.

When individuals open themselves up like this on the internet it makes people more likely to buy products from them because they have already established a relationship with their viewers.

I am not saying that you must produce vlogs if you want to be successful on the internet, although you most certainly can if you want, but I am saying that it is important to learn from how others have found success and use those people as an inspiration for what you want to do and the spin you may want to put on their kind of brand.

Let's use an example to make things a little clearer. Say that you own a wool blanket company and you sell your blankets mainly for camping and cold weather. You might produce videos of yourself and some friends going camping with your blankets, showing how useful one of your blankets can be for a cold night underneath the stars. You could also include videos about how you make your blankets, showing where you get the wool from, how you spin the wool, and how you weave the fibers together to produce the final product.

By including so much detail about the product you are selling and how someone might use your product, you are able to communicate as much information as possible to your customers and establish a relationship with them that you can't do as well with a simple website.

You can extend your personal brand of wool blankets to other social media platforms, sharing pictures of yourself using your blankets, possibly including customer testimonials from people who have enjoyed using your blankets. You could offer deals to people through

Facebook or Instagram, ensuring that people remain followers of you on these various platforms.

By showing that you, yourself, use your products and that other customers have enjoyed using them as well, you can easily sell more products to more people than you would be able to do having not used such platforms.

As I have said before, the power of YouTube and other social media sites is that it creates a more personal platform through which you can establish relationships with your customers. I remind you of this not to simply be repetitive, but because this is the single most important thing to understand about a site like YouTube. It gives you the opportunity to show your customers who you are as a person and not just as the guy who sells them a product.

Exposing yourself to potentially millions of viewers can be challenging, and those who are shy or introverted may find it difficult to overcome their fears, but remember that you will not overcome this fear by waiting around and doing nothing. You will find it much easier to overcome these fears by simply going out and producing videos. Personally, I found that my fears of being seen by so many potential viewers had gone away completely after uploading only a couple of videos. You will probably have a similar experience.

As we have learned earlier in this book, commitment is essential to success, and that we must dive right into our projects if we are to make the most of the time and resources we have at our disposal. One of the biggest reasons so many people put off starting their own YouTube channel is their fear of putting themselves out there, but just keep in mind your goals and your potential for success and you will be able to follow through with your plans and hopefully end up as successful as you want to be.

If you really aren't ready to expose yourself to this kind of attention yet, you can always start by producing videos that don't feature you in them at all and work your way up. You could produce a video that just has a couple of pictures and music in it, then make a video that you narrate, and then make a video that you are included in. This way you can slowly get more and more involved in the videos you are trying to produce.

In terms of production, do not think that you need the best equipment or any really expensive software when you are just starting out. Many successful YouTubers have made a fortune without any investment into equipment at all, simply using their phone's camera and microphone.

This type of production setup can look unprofessional if you don't know what you are doing, but if you understand basic principles about lighting and speaking clearly enough to be audible, then you shouldn't need really expensive equipment to get started. There's also plenty of free software that provide a good alternative to expensive video editors.

When your YouTube channel grows and more and more people begin watching your videos you may want to invest in a high-quality camera, microphone, and editing software, but this is not required when you are just starting out.

Another thing you should consider when starting your YouTube channel is how much of a time commitment may be involved. You can easily produce a video a day with only an hour or two involved in filming and editing, but you will likely spend many more hours than that speaking with people on social media, responding to questions about your products, and working on future content, so it is important to appropriately budget your time.

Developing a successful brand using YouTube will require time and dedication, but the rewards of using this platform are endless. Imagine how many people you will be able to reach when you effectively use YouTube; imagine how many products you will be able to sell by harnessing all of the tools at your disposal.

There are so many things that make YouTube a viable platform for the development of your brand, so many, in fact, that it impossible to cover them all in this book. My advice to anyone who is interested in using YouTube would be to spend as much time on their website in the coming weeks and try learning as much about it as possible. Learn how others have used YouTube to develop their brands, the kind of tools YouTube provides its creators with for monetization, advertising, and brand interaction. There are many YouTube channels that offer advice on how to make money on YouTube, although few discuss personal branding as in depth as this book. It will be through using the advice on personal branding you have learned in this book that will give you the appropriate lens through which you can learn more about YouTube.

The purpose of this book is not to tell you exactly how to produce videos, how to market those videos, how to respond to unfavorable comments about your videos, or how to monetize your videos on YouTube. This book is here to orient you towards success by revealing the power of personal branding. You can learn how to produce videos from someone else. You can learn how long your videos should be, how to use clickbait, and how to grow your channel from someone else. What no one else will teach you about, however, is the importance of personal branding on the internet, and especially how you should develop your YouTube channel, your Amazon page, or you Blog, so that your personal brand is effectively marketed.

What I have told you in this chapter cannot be understood unless you go and interact with YouTube in some way. Watch videos, take notes, participate in livestreams, explore other's personal brands and learn from all that they are doing. The best way to learn is by doing.

It will only be once you do these things that you come to appreciate the lessons contained in this chapter and the entire book in general. With the information I have provided you so far you can now appreciate the videos on YouTube in an entirely new way. Instead of watching a video and seeing it as a purely entertaining piece, you may find yourself wondering how much money their channel makes a month, what kind of product they sell on their website, how many Facebook or Twitter followers their business has, and how they cooperate with other channels to make more money.

Use this information to your advantage and begin to see the videos you watch in a different light, as the businesses and personal brands they probably are. This isn't a cynical perspective, but rather, an uplifting position through which you can better appreciate your chances for success online.

Chapter Eight:
The Blogging Market

Much like YouTube, the blogging market is built around personal brands. Blogging is an especially personal way for businesses to communicate with their customers and it can be much easier to start than a YouTube channel.

Blogging has been one of the most popular ways to make money online for decades now. All you need to make a blog is a computer and some basic writing skills. Because of this, anyone interested in starting an online business who is concerned about start-up costs should consider writing a blog as a way of wading into the online business market.

Blogs can be about anything that interests you, whether that be sports, gardening, fashion, woodworking, art collecting, or something else. You can even begin blogging as a hobby, without any initial attempts at monetizing your brand.

Blogging is not the quickest way to grow to a large company, though, and it could take a year or more before your blog is popular enough to support a full-time income, so understand this before you get involved.

The advantage to blogging, however, is that the time involved in starting a blog is minimal. You can begin by writing a couple of posts a week, maybe taking four or five hours every week to work on your blog. Once you get into the groove of writing a couple of times a week you'll find it easier to post more often, possibly even working up to posting several times a day if your blog is successful enough.

Like YouTube, blogs will achieve more success in a shorter period of time if you actively post as much as you can on a regular schedule. I would suggest posting at least three times a week when you are just starting, as this shouldn't take more than an hour each day (remember the exercise in chapter one about taking an hour each day and working?). When you build a following, you can start posting more frequently and offer your fans more content.

Blogs can also be an easy way to expand an existing brand to even more markets. If you already have a personal brand developed on YouTube, you can post every day on your blog and give your followers even more exposure to yourself and your brand. Because blogging offers an alternative medium with which you can showcase your brand, it can serve you well in expanding your existing customer base to those who prefer more traditional communication.

In many ways blogs act similarly to YouTube or any other personal branding outlet you can think of. They allow users to interact with the content through commenting on articles, receiving exclusive content through email lists, and through the products you sell. This is what makes blogging such a useful tool for your online business, as it is relatively easy to do and can be done as an extension to your existing brand.

I want to point out that a blog doesn't necessarily have to be separate from your brand's website, in fact, it might be best if it is on the same site. A blog merely acts as a way of communicating information and content to your fans and customers. This is similar to a YouTube video in its intent; simply done through different means.

A blog, although it offers huge potential as an extension to an existing brand, can also be used as the main platform through which you can sell your products or services.

Let's use the example of a fashion blog. You may write about current trends in men's fashion, updating your fans about new and exciting products and styles that your customers are interested in. It will serve you well to be ready to sell your customers any new products that surface in the industry, like a creative hair-gel or colorful socks.

If you can establish yourself as someone who knows what they're talking about when it comes to men's fashion, you can use that to sell products that have to do with men's fashion. The trust you've built by establishing your brand will help sell your products.

If you become very successful you can even influence that market in your favor, coming up with a new idea for jeans or belts and sell your product as the "newest thing" in men's fashion. Once you demonstrate yourself to be a reputable source for fashion advice, you will be able to develop your own trends in favor of the products you sell.

This is true about your personal brand in general, but blogging offers a different kind of setting in which you can develop your brand towards this kind of goal.

A blog is much like a newspaper or magazine. It can be both formal and informal at the same time. Think of the content that you are sharing with your followers. It is written and not video; organized and not stream of consciousness. This makes blogging one of the most trust-producing platforms for your brand. It can make your brand seem professional and reliable. This professionalism and reliability is enhanced when you present your blog in a thought-out, high quality manner; produced with regularity.

This isn't to say that a blog needs to be extremely formal if you don't want it to be. Some very successful blogs have been produced with little attention to detail, accentuating its "common-man" feel. If this sort of style sounds like it would go well with the niche that you are operating within, then go for it, but it is fair to say that the biggest advantage of a blog is that it conveys professionalism in a way that you can't do on another platform without considerable investment.

This goes back to the biggest advantage of blogging over other markets. A website can cost as little as $10-20 when you're just starting out, and all a blog really needs is a website and a writer.

If you are at all a competent writer, then your blog's success will generate itself. All you need to do is write consistently and with a direction to your brand. It will be easy for you to gain a following if you properly implement the techniques we have discussed throughout this book. Remember that you serve your customers just as much as they serve you and you should be just fine.

Do not wait to start your blog. You can start blogging now and develop your brand later if you want. Because blogging is such a promising market to develop you brand in, often times your brand will develop itself to some extent as you continue sharing content with your customers and begin to learn about those customers and the things they are interested in.

I would suggest that you start writing your blog today if you think this is the market you want to operate in. Take out a piece of paper and something to write with and write down things that you are interested in discussing in your blog. This may already have been taken care of if you wrote down your goals in the first chapter, as you can easily use your goals as a starting point for your blog.

Write for as long as you feel comfortable, and once you're done you will likely have the first blog-post that you can share.

It can take a while to develop a following through your blog alone, although you can certainly become successful without anything besides a simple blog. It will be important that you understand the rest of the internet market before you begin your blog, because you will definitely interact with other online businesses once you start a blog, so don't write-off the rest of this book if you feel that blogging is the right fit for you. Hopefully the next few chapters will give you a solid understanding of the rest of the internet market and how it can affect you and your brand.

Remember that the internet markets are all connected in many ways. If you choose one particular market to operate within you will need to understand other markets in order to recognize opportunities and anticipate change.

Chapter Nine:
The Freelance Market

When developing your personal brand, you will likely outsource some of the work you need done for your business. This is where freelancing will come into play.

Freelancing involves someone selling their skills in a particular field to a customer who needs something made for them. A good example would be logo-design. If you don't know anything about graphic design you will want to hire someone to design a logo for you, and you can do this by going online and hiring a person to design it for you. You may end up paying a small fee of $50 or $100 for your logo, but you end up with a quality logo that you can use to market your brand.

It is worth noting that the freelancing market can be extremely profitable if you are particularly good at a certain skill. If you are a really good graphic designer, have a degree in music, can write a book in five hours, then you might consider offering your services to customers online. There are many freelancers who make tens-of-thousands of dollars a month selling their skills to customers who ask them to produce something for them.

If you are like most people and don't know much about graphic design, music production, or some other skill, then you really shouldn't try selling your services to people on freelance websites, because the competition is considerably higher than in any other market. This competition can serve you well as an online business owner, though, because competition lowers prices on things.

Think about the logo-design example I mentioned. While $50 to $100 might seem sort of high for a simple logo design, there was a time when logo design could have cost you several hundred or several thousand dollars or more. It is the competition that exists in the freelance market that makes prices so low, and this will lower costs for you as a business owner.

Although prices will be lower than they might otherwise be, competition means that there are literally thousands of freelancers that you will need to choose from to get the product you want.

You will need to recognize which freelancers are the best ones to use, and this will often be about finding a balance between quality and price.

Never choose freelancers simply because of their price. Those who offer the best prices may be able to produce quality work but will often be difficult to communicate with and won't end up being worth the money if they don't give you the product that you are looking for.

As you will most likely be able to see or listen to a freelancer's portfolio before you hire them for the job, you need to be skeptical that the seemingly good quality work that they have produced for their portfolio is something they will be able to replicate for your project. Just because you like the work they have done in the past doesn't mean that you can depend on them to produce something of similar quality again.

You will find that hiring the right freelancer will be the most difficult task involved in this market. In my own personal experience, there have been quite a few freelance artists who have exceptional credentials, even from Ivy League colleges, who are simply not right for the job. Sometimes this is because they will take too long to produce a product, other times it will be because there is a language barrier involved (many freelancers live overseas), and other times they aren't good at communicating ideas over email or over the phone.

I once hired an American freelancer who had graduated from a good school, had high quality examples from previous works of his, and even included a small bio telling me about the work he enjoys doing and a little bit about himself. He seemed like the right man for the job, so I hired him. He assured me that it wouldn't take him more than 48 hours to finish the job. However, after 24 hours had passed, he showed me the less than stellar work he had done so far; I knew that I probably should have spent more time finding a better freelancer to hire. He ended up spending nearly a week working on the project, and in the end I was not entirely satisfied with the work he had done.

Learn from my mistake here. Spend time finding the right fit for your project, even if it means forking over a little extra money, because when everything is finished you will have saved yourself time and effort on your part.

Finding the balance between quality and price will require a learning curve on your part. The amount of competition in the freelance market means that there are more than enough high-quality freelancers out there, but it also means that there are even more bad ones who will waste your time and money and leave you dissatisfied with the final product.

Most projects you want done shouldn't cost you more than one-hundred dollars. You can find really good freelancers for even less than that depending on the project, but remember that it is difficult to find such people, and sometimes it's best to go with the freelancer who is clearly reputable, spend the extra cash, and get a good quality product in a short amount of time.

Being able to recognize the right freelancers for the job will take practice, but with time you will begin to understand the market, possibly finding a freelancer you can return to for most of your projects.

If you have the money, you may even consider outsourcing most of the work for your brand to freelancers. Find one you can count on for quality work, pay him or her for each project you need finished, and spend less time producing your own content and focus on selling that content. This type of business structure will cost much more money upfront, and this shouldn't be considered if you can't afford it, but this can save you a lot of time in the long run and can allow you to produce more content in a shorter period of time. Find one or two freelancers you trust and hire them to produce content for your brand, almost turning them into an extension of your business. Establish a relationship with them, allow them flexibility as they produce content for you, and work towards marketing the content they make for you. I know of many successful internet businessmen who have effectively used this technique to their advantage as they manage a large personal brand and expand that brand rapidly to success.

Again, this technique should not be used if you cannot afford it. I simply mean to illustrate how useful freelancers can be in the development of your brand. When you need something produced for your personal brand, whether that be a logo, a jingle, an advertisement, animation, or even videos or books, you should always consider using freelancers to produce the content for you. You should only do this, though, if the time you save not having to do these tasks yourself will be well spent producing other aspects of your brand. While it is possible to pay others to produce all content for your brand and just sit there while other people make you rich, this requires monumental startup costs. When you are just beginning an online business, however, you will find that occasionally outsourcing work will afford you the time to produce other content that will add to your brand, rendering the costs associated with hiring a freelancer completely worth it. It's important that you find this balance, between not wasting too much money on freelancers, and outsourcing some work to free up your time to develop your business.

SECTION FOUR:
Start Your Business

Chapter Ten:
Finding Your Niche

Now that you have come to understand the online business market you can now understand everything that will be involved in developing and marketing your personal brand.

Critically important to the success of your brand will be finding the right niche to operate in. This will involve choosing the appropriate market in which you want to operate and focusing your interests into a specific circle that you are familiar with.

A niche, in its literal definition refers, to a space designated for a particular object or ornament. You can think of an online business niche as a space designated for your brand; it is something unique to you and your brand.

A properly located niche allows you adequate wiggle room in which to develop and sell your personal brand. It is, therefore, essential that you choose the right niche.

You can begin this process by reviewing the goals you set forth in the first chapter of this book. Knowing how you want your life to look in twenty-five years can help you immensely in your search for an appropriate niche. When you recognize aspects of your character that may fit into a particular niche, then you will be able to choose a niche that works with the goals that you have laid out.

We have identified three macro-markets within the online business world that give you a foundation for your personal brand, and within these macro-markets we have located micro-markets that you can operate in.

1. The Amazon Market
    - Amazon FBA
2. The YouTube Market
    - Personal Branding
3. The Blogging Market
    - Personal Branding

Personal branding isn't a micro-market in itself, but rather, it contains those micro-markets that you will want to explore when making the choice as to which niche works best for you. Understand that there are literally thousands of micro-markets that you may want to look into, like fashion, cooking, working out, entrepreneurship, writing, sports, or history to name just a handful.

Within these micro-markets you will find the niches that will interest you and help you develop the essential customer base you need. In the micro-market of fashion on YouTube, you can choose niches like shoes, jackets, historical trends, current trends, world trends, wearing hats, fashion etiquette, and many more.

As you choose a niche you intend to work in you should work in steps to find that niche:

1. Which macro-market interests you most?
    a. Amazon?
    b. YouTube?
    c. Blogging?
    d. All three?

2. Taking a look at your goals, and thinking about your interests, which micro-market makes the most sense for you?
    a. Fashion?
    b. Cooking
    c. Exercise?
    d. Entrepreneurship?
    e. Writing?
    f. Sports?
    g. History?
    h. Education?
    i. Science?
    j. Something else?

3. Within the micro-market, what possible niches exist?

You must know that niches don't necessarily already exist, nor is it always possible to find an existing niche without specifically looking for it. Take the niche of personal branding itself. Although most successful people on the internet use personal branding to their advantage, there are few people who openly discuss its use in business because it is so important. The niche of personal branding is a closely guarded one that few people know about, and even fewer capitalize on. You should always be on the lookout for potential niches during your daily life, because this will allow to swiftly build a personal brand around that niche.

Do not be mistaken as to what niches you should be looking for, however. Do not find a niche that is so small that only a few thousand people would ever be interested in it. You also shouldn't find a niche that is too large and oversaturated. A niche that will serve you well is something that is underappreciated. If you are interested in sports, for example, do not start a YouTube channel about football, as so many people already do this. Instead, you can focus your niche on, let's say, football oriented video games, or children's football toys, or the medical risks associated with the sport. Each of these particular niches are football oriented (a subsection of a micro-market), and the niche that you choose is even more focused than that and can incorporate other things that interest you. If you like football and video games, then you can develop a personal brand around playing football video games. If you have children and enjoy playing football with them and taking them to games, then you could create a personal brand around that niche, and sell products to people in a similar situation to your own.

You can now see how your own interest in a subject can help sell products for you. If you are a parent who plays football with your children you can easily establish an online relationship with other parents who do the same, and with that relationship you can sell products that you know your customers will want.

As we have learned previously, the success of your personal brand is contingent on your interest for the niche in which your brand operates. You cannot establish trust with your customers, and therefore, sell more products, if you do not understand your customers on a personal level.

This is why choosing a niche will be one of the most important parts of your journey to success. If you are not interested in the niche you pick you will not be successful.

My advice to you is to spend time searching for your niche. Finding the right niche will take time. Sometimes you will know exactly which niche you want to focus on right from the start, other times it might take you weeks, months, or even years before you can recognize the appropriate niche for you.

You can use the information contained in this book to your advantage in finding a niche and hopefully expedited your search for one. The chapter on commitment can be helpful in reminding you to spend as much of your day as possible in awareness of markets at play in the world around you.

When you are committed to success, as we learned in the second chapter, you become aware of how things operate and how money changes hands around us all the time. Once you develop this awareness you will be able to quickly recognize business opportunities everywhere you go, and now that you are armed with even more information about how the online market operates, you will be able to recognize patterns in all your internet surfing.

Before you jump into starting your business you need to find the absolute best niche for you and the brand you want to create. This will take time, commitment, and awareness, but once you locate the right niche for you, you will be well prepared for success.

This takes us back to the first chapter, where we discussed the meaning of success and how much effort it will take to create it. If the first step to creating success is defining your goals, then one of the next steps is discovering a niche that will work for you, your goals, and your business. In the next chapter we will discuss how to orient your business for success, but before you can do that you will need to have as good an understanding about the business you want to create as possible. Using what you have learned in the past few chapters you will soon be able to create a successful business that will lead you to the achievement of all those goals you wrote down in the first chapter, but understand that you are approaching the final stages of preparation in your business. Soon you will jump right into the online marketplace, selling yourself and your brand to customers, but you don't want to do this hastily.

It is critical before you take the leap and invest time and money into your business, that you step back and look at the big picture once more.

I would like to share the following anecdote with you about Henry Kissinger that I think illustrates my point well:

When Henry Kissinger was Secretary of State he asked one of his assistants to write a formal report on the developing situation in the Middle East. The assistant quickly got to work writing the twenty-page report and by the next morning he had finished the report and left it on Kissinger's desk. The assistant found the report back on his own desk within a couple of hours with the words "Is this really your best work?" written on the top of the page. He sat back down in front of his typewriter and worked for hours before he again put the report on Kissinger's desk. The next day he found the paper returned to him once more, with the same words written on the front: "Is this really your best work?" So he rewrote the report and once again left it on Kissinger's desk. As the assistant was about to leave for the day he found the report back on his desk with the same words written on the front. He stormed into Kissinger's office and exclaimed "Yes, dammit! Yes! This really is my best work!" With that Kissinger slowly sat up in his chair, smiling, and said "Well then, I suppose I'll read it this time."

What this story demonstrates is that there are always things that can be improved about something. Just as the assistant was not finished with his report until the third time, you shouldn't consider yourself ready to start your business until you are 100% certain that you have researched everything you need to and planned everything for any eventuality.

Although there is only so much you can plan for in advance, you need to be as secure in your venture as possible so as not to take any unnecessary risks. You will find that there are many things to learn about the business world that can only be learned from experiencing it first-hand, but preparing for everything as best as you can will serve you well.

Finding the right niche for your brand is essential to a successful online business, and I hope that this book has helped you so far in your journey towards success. The next step is, of course, creating your business, and for that you must be prepared to take on a massive amount of work.

If you are at all skeptical about your chances for success, remember that the only thing standing in the way of your success is you. You must commit to success in order to be successful. So if you are ready to start your business, continue onto the next chapter where we will solidify the information we have covered so far and set your plans in motion for the creation of a business that will give you the tools with which you will set yourself up for a successful life.

Chapter Eleven:
Framing Your Business for Success

Throughout the course of this book you have learned about the online marketplace and how you can use it to your advantage in business. Before you go out and start an online business for yourself there are some preparatory things you must do.

In the beginning of this book we discussed the two types of goals you can create for yourself—personal and business—and showed how there is often overlap between the two. It is essential to understand that the work you do for your business will become part of your life and your personal success will largely be wedded to your business success.

Many people will invest thousands of dollars into their business only to see it fail within a couple of years. They shamefully crawl back to their former employers and beg for their old job back, swearing that they will never do anything so stupid as starting their own business again. Never do this.

If your business fails, remember that it was your first try at a business. If your second business fails, remember that it was only your second try at a business. If your one-hundredth business fails, remember that it was only your hundredth try. Each time you make a mistake in the business world you learn more about how not to do certain things, and that kind of negative knowledge is often more important to know than any other kind. Remember that few people are successful the first time.

Knowing what *to do* is important, but knowing what *not to do* is even more important. It is this negative knowledge that will allow you to immediately shut down any bad ideas you or someone else has about how to run your business. Negative knowledge is something that is best acquired through personal experience, and so it will be difficult for me to give you any negative knowledge myself. I will say, however, to *never* give up.

Many of the most successful people on earth have only come to their success after many failures, and it would be difficult to find anyone who has found success on their first try. So it is important that you don't see failure as a sign that you won't be successful. Failure is, essentially, the first step to success. It shows you that things won't come as easily as you may have initially thought, and that it is only through dedication and hard work that your success will be realized.

I want to challenge you, once you finish reading this book, to start a business. Not next month, not next week, but the very minute you put down this book. As we have established, it takes personal experience to show the best path to take, and you can only gain personal experience from doing, not from sitting around waiting for success to come to you.

Spend the next few days and weeks developing a business. Keep track of ideas you have, make note of your goals, and be on the lookout for potential niches that you may want to work in. Take as much time out of your day as you can to do this, and within a few weeks you will find yourself on the path to success.

Remember that success is not found, but created. It is created by hard work, dedication, and sacrifice. In the coming weeks you will lay the groundwork for your success by working as hard as you can.

Starting your business will require serious preparation, and you have already taken steps to preparation by reading this book. Filled with new information about the online market you will be able to better formulate your business for success.

Spend time researching the markets more, calculate potential expenses, and speak with industry experts about their own successes and failures in that market. Write down any information you think might be necessary and remember that you can't be over-prepared.

When you feel that you are ready to start your business you should already be filled with as much information as possible. Do not wait to research things until after you start your business, but find out as much as you can now about the market you want to work in and the customers you will need support from.

Remember that the single most important thing to finding success online is developing a personal brand. Your brand will act as the bridge between you and your customers and will allow you to sell more products to more people.

If you do not create a personal brand, then you will not be able to create success. There are some businessmen who have not used personal branding in their business and have been successful, but they stumbled upon success and did not create it; they got lucky. The best advice anyone can give you about online success is on creating a personal brand. Few people discuss it because it is essential to their own success and are afraid to share their secrets.

If you want to frame your business for success you need to look at your business as an extension of yourself. This is why it will require so much hard work and sacrifice, because it will become like a child to you and children need more attention than anything else.

It is because of this that you need to be certain of your intentions. When you doubt yourself, your chances of success diminish and you consequently find yourself on even less stable ground.

Remember how we used the metaphor of the internet market as a jungle? Just as you would never wander into a jungle without the right equipment, you will need to be as prepared as possible for your journey into the world of business. You will likely be on your own out there, so you'll need all of the protection you can get, and protection comes through preparation.

After you prepare yourself for success you will actually start your business. You may be disappointed with the initial results; slow viewer traffic, few, if any, sales, and a couple of dissatisfied customers. Do not take this as a sign that your business is failing, especially if you happen to make any money at all. Success doesn't happen overnight; your brand will take time to start to be successful.

Let's say you make $50 your first week of business when you had expected to make $200. Far from being bad news, this tells you that the product you are selling is valued by someone, meaning that with a better business plan you could make even more sales, potentially surpassing any expectations you had. If you didn't make any money at all, recognize that there is likely something wrong with your product, and then fix it.

Don't sit around waiting for sales to come, do something to make them happen. Before you actually start your business all your work should be focused on research and development, but once you do start your business you should start working towards more sales over anything else, and as we learned in chapter five, sales are driven by the relationship you have with your customers.

Within the first few weeks of starting your business you should be able to see how successful your business plan will be. If there are problems, you will need to fix them. Sometimes the idea you have for a product or personal brand is great, but the only thing holding you back is your production quality; what you will need to do is ask your customers how you can improve your product and then improve it.

In the business world there is a concept of continuous improvement. This means being constantly on the lookout for ways to improve your business, your product, and your brand. The most successful companies of all time use this concept every day and are always analyzing their work for ways to improve themselves.

You, also, will need to be continuously improving your business. You will not be successful right from the start, but rather, you will need to spend time reviewing what you have done and asking yourself serious questions about your business and how you can improve it. This goes back to the anecdote about Henry Kissinger in the last chapter; you will need to be asking yourself every day "is this *really* my best work?" If it *really* is your best work than give yourself a high five and keep working, but if it isn't, then you will need to spend the time to improve it. You cannot create a successful business without producing the highest quality products and content that you are capable of producing.

When you learn to be always improving the quality of your work your business will be more successful. It is as simple as that.

You will come to realize, as you wade into the waters of the online marketplace, that it will be your commitment to your goals that will provide you the best chances for success.

Use the goals that you wrote down in the first chapter as encouragement towards success. Look at the list every day and remind yourself of what you are trying to achieve. There will be times when you want to quit, but this reminder will deter you from that kind of mistake.

Your success can be only a few months to years away if you want it to be. Do not settle for a life that is less than successful, but be always striving for the best that you and your business can be. It is up to you to achieve the level of success that you want to achieve, so I encourage you, today, to go out and get to work on your business. You are now equipped with enough information to get started on your business, and with the proper dedication you will soon be able to achieve every goal you make for yourself and live the life that you want to live.

www.ingramcontent.com/pod-product-compliance
Lightning Source LLC
Chambersburg PA
CBHW070310230526
45470CB00002B/808